Monica – Congratu
success & your c
GTC 2015 "Unstop,
I believe in you!
Love ya!
ERVP Carolyn McCockle

How To Believe In Yourself:
A 7-Step Guide For Overcoming Fear and Self-Doubt

Carmen Parks

Monica,
Believe in yourself & go for it!
Carm M Parks

DEDICATION

I dedicate this book to my Mom and my business/writing coach. Without the two of them this book wouldn't have been written. Before settling on a topic, I had fears and reservations about sharing my story. These two amazing women helped me find the courage to believe in myself in order to make this book a reality.

I also dedicate this book to all those who have dreams and desires for their future. May you learn how to trust your instincts and always believe in yourself.

CONTENTS

1 INTRODUCTION

"Believe in yourself, and the rest will fall into place. Have faith in your own abilities, work hard, and there is nothing you cannot accomplish." ~Brad Henry

You have chosen to read this book because either you, or someone you know, can benefit by overcoming fear and/or self-doubt. Whether you are a manager, executive, student, self-employed, young, old, or somewhere in between, the information provided in this book can have a major impact on the way you think about your ability to reach your goals.

This book is designed for your own personal development if any of the following apply:

1. You have goals but also experience doubt about your ability to reach your goals.
2. You fear failing because of past failures.
3. You have a tendency to second guess yourself.
4. You see obstacles standing in your way when you really want to achieve something.
5. You tend to have excuses for why things can't be the way you want them to be.

You may have read books and articles that provide suggestions and tips for believing in yourself. This book is a step-by step guide that takes you from where you are now to where you want to be. This seven-step process provides more than just tips. This process requires you to pay attention to what is really going on inside of your mind and your body.

There are hundreds of examples in literature that explain to you the importance of believing in yourself. Short excerpts, that I've found useful, are shared in this book. There is no single way to believe in yourself. My hope is that you are able to gain a clearer perspective of who you are and where you want to go in life.

M. Farouk Radwan wrote: "Believe in Yourself and People Will Be Forced To Believe In You" He shares the following introduction:

"It's All About Believing in Yourself. Have you ever seen someone who didn't buy a car because he failed to learn how to drive? Or have you ever met someone who tried to learn how to drive then decided not to try again after failing a few times?

Personally, I have never met anyone like that. Almost everyone who starts learning how to drive ends up being able to drive well. Although not everyone becomes a driving expert, still everyone who tries, learns the basics of this complex skill.

The question is, why you succeeded in learning how to drive yet failed in achieving some of your other goals?

The answer is simple: because you were sure that you were going to be able to drive long before you sat in the driver's seat. You saw everyone around you succeeding in doing it and so were convinced that there's nothing particularly hard about it, even though it really is a complicated skill."

M. Farouk Radwan makes a very important point. Those that are successful first believe they can reach their goals. Therefore, the first step to achieving any goal is believing in yourself. If you don't actually believe you can reach your goal, then chances are, it won't happen. Why? Well as it was said in the movie the "The Santa Clause" with Tim Allen "Seeing isn't believing, believing is seeing." When you believe you can accomplish your goals, you are able to actually see yourself in the future achieving that goal. You picture it and visualize it but most importantly you experience it over and over and over in your head until it actually happens.

I am deeply saddened when I hear about someone who gives up on something they really want. Instead, they end up settling for less because they didn't believe they could achieve their goal. Life is too short to settle! Whether you think you can, or you think you can't, you are right. This is the very definition of the phrase 'self-fulfilling prophecy.'

Let's look at this from a different perspective. Are you someone who doubts yourself, or in other words, do you have a tendency to say, I can't do it, only to find that you couldn't actually do it? You told yourself "Nope, that's not going to happen for me," and sure enough it didn't happen. What you believed to be true about yourself did actually come true. The outcome you pictured, was the outcome you experienced. What if you take all of that energy you use to talk down to yourself, and instead you use it to empower yourself? Your self-talk can actually lead you to believe in yourself and to believe what you set your mind to achieve.

Visualizations and tapping into your internal power are key to implementing this seven-step process. A visualization is an image, picture or movie that you play in your mind as you imagine outcomes to future events.

Your internal power is your own personal energy. You share and manifest your energy through your feelings and emotions. You may not have known it at the time, but you have already used your internal power to make your visualizations come true. Those visualizations are what you have expected to occur in the future. When you add your own personal energy (your feelings or emotions) to your visualizations, you give them life.

For example, you didn't get the job, you did get caught in traffic, you didn't finish the race, you didn't lose the weight. You visualized yourself not reaching your goals and guess what, you didn't reach your goals. When you had those visualizations, you also experienced some sort of emotion or feeling. Those feelings are your internal power. Isn't it time that you started using your visualizations and internal power to help you reach your goals?

Melissa Ng wrote an article titled "How to Believe in Yourself in the Face of Overwhelming Self-Doubt." She outlines her story and shares:

> *"When I was a child, I was in love with drawing. For me, drawing was as exciting as going to the playground. At some point in my childhood, I decided I'd become an artist of some kind. But the critics in my life were quick to cut me down. I'll bet you've heard the same kind of clichés:*
>
> *"Art is great but not a 'realistic' future goal. While it's a nice hobby to have, you can't really make a living out of it. You'll just be another starving artist."*

Melissa goes on to share how she internalized the words many people expressed to her and even as an adult she continued to talk herself out of her dream to be an artist.

Fear and self-doubt are emotions we all experience in one form or another. My experiences in life have been a little bit different. I have been very fortunate and have been able to reach every concrete, tangible goal that I've set my mind to achieve. I am referring to the big stuff. This includes: graduating with the degrees I wanted with the GPA I wanted, landing the job I wanted after college and finishing running races as I planned. However, I struggle with reaching goals that require me to be emotionally vulnerable. Writing this book, and sharing my story require me to turn off the seventh grade naysayers and simply take the plunge.

Before I started writing this book and committed to sharing my story and my beliefs, I kept replaying the words of my seventh grade friends. I was made fun of for being smart. I was teased for getting A's in math. I wasn't very popular because of the belief that most girls aren't good at math. In middle school I had a hard time fitting in with the cool kids. Until recently, I didn't realize that those comments affected the way I thought about myself and my personal achievements.

When I did reach my goals, the previously mentioned degrees and races, those things didn't just happen. After planning and hard work, it took months and years of executing and adjusting a pre-designed plan. However, the one thing that remained the same in all of those instances is that I knew what I wanted and I put all of my energy into pursuing that one option.

However, when it comes to being vulnerable, I do have a tendency to doubt myself and I have, on many occasions, used my thoughts to talk myself out of what I wanted because it didn't seem rational or reasonable. Throughout my life there have been opportunities that I didn't take advantage of because I had other goals that I was working toward. The key is to be clear and decisive and know that your heart will lead you in the right direction.

I use different strategies for staying motivated, however, when I really, really want something, I make it happen, because I believe I can. When I want to reach my goal/desire, I have mental systems in place that prevent me from talking myself out of what I want. However, I also have thoughts that include excuses. I have learned to recognize my excuses, reevaluate and then make the decision that best serves my goals.

One very important process I've learned is to stop the thoughts that result in second guessing the outcome. That way, the outcome is always the same as the initial visualization. This desired outcome keeps me motivated. I truly believe that if I want to achieve something, I can. I don't want to achieve every possible goal available, but the outcomes that I have chosen, I have been able to experience. In my mind, my desired outcome is the only option.

So how does this work, why do I think this way and how can you learn how to do it too? It takes practice. Thought patterns are habits. I believe that I learned by example from my parents and I quite possibly received some great ideas from children's books. Dr. Seuss states the following in his best-selling children's book <u>Oh The Places You Will Go</u>:

> *"You have brains in your head. You have feet in your shoes. You can steer yourself any direction you choose. You're on your own. And you know what you know. And YOU are the one who'll decide where to go."*

Maybe, without knowing it, my parents provided the tools I needed, through simple Dr. Seuss rhymes. I also learned from experience. I didn't always recognize what I was doing, I just knew that I was able to reach my goals. Now I know that consistency is key and every single day I use the practices outlined in this book. These steps always come in handy, especially if I am on a quest to achieve something I've never done before.

Successfully completing the exercises outlined in this book require you to be truly honest with yourself. Please be willing to write down your true honest thoughts about yourself and your situation. Once your thoughts are "on the table" you will have the opportunity to analyze them and decide if you want to continue to have those thoughts.

According to several studies, those who take personal responsibility for their situations tend to be happier and more successful. Therefore, taking personal responsibility for your thoughts is a necessity if you are going to believe in yourself. You and you alone are responsible for your thoughts. No one threatens your life and says, "you must think this way." You have the choice, we all have the choice to choose our thoughts.

As I look back at my achievements, I now have a different perspective regarding my previous successes. Without recognizing what I was doing at the time, there are a few processes that led me to effectively reach my goals. Only recently have I recognized that there is a formula to follow.

1. **Really, really want it** – If you don't really, really want it, the process is a lot harder to execute.

2. **Visualize yourself achieving it** – See yourself making your dreams come true.

3. **Create a plan** – Not having a plan is like going on a treasure hunt without a map.

4. **Create a mantra or affirmation** – This is something you say to yourself over and over and over until you actually reach your goal. Having an uplifting, motivating statement leaves little room for outside fears and thoughts, because nothing else is true except for your mantra.

5. **Take Action** – You can only reach your goals if you take steps in the direction of your desired outcome.

I want to share with you that the life I'm living now, I visualized more than two years ago. Not all of the details were crystal clear, but by letting go of many of my excuses, I was able to make decisions that led me to where I am today.

So you might ask: "what am I supposed to visualize?" Remember that believing is seeing. What you see in your visualization is what comes true in real life. You already use this wonderful skill to visualize what you don't want to happen. Your expectations of failure and fear of lack of ability tend to come true right?

So how do you go from having self-doubt to believing in yourself no matter what? That is a pretty big step and it starts with your thoughts. This book is designed to be a step-by-step guide, to help you experience different thoughts and the feelings associated with those thoughts. You always get to choose your thoughts. If you want to continue to have self-defeating thoughts and excuses as to why you can't reach your goals, then this book is not for you and I suggest you put it down right now. Stop reading if self-defeat is what you want to continue to experience for the rest of your life.

If you are ready to learn how to change your thoughts, create mantras/affirmations/declarations and visualize your way to your goals then keep on reading! By putting these lessons to use you will feel more empowered, capable and accomplished as you work toward any outcome or goal that you choose.

Are you ready to start believing in yourself? Let's do this!

CARMEN PARKS

2 SELECT A GOAL/OUTCOME/DESIRE

As Lisa Nichols says in the Book <u>The Secret</u>
"The first step is to ask. Make a command to the universe. Let the universe know what you want. The universe responds to your thoughts."

Step 1 is all about identifying what you really, really want. This is also the first step in applying the concept of The Secret. If you don't know what you want, how are you going to know what to think, how to feel about it and what steps to take to get there? You must first identify what you want. This is something that you may have reservations about, whether it is a fear of failure, not knowing where to start, or you may be doubting yourself or doubting your ability to actually achieve it.

We all have different ideas about what we want out of life and what we want to experience. Sometimes we don't ever take an outside perspective when we are making these big decisions.

My big life change was choosing to leave my position as a Professional Civil Engineer, go back to school and become a Wellness Practitioner. I didn't know how I was going to make it work. All I knew is that I couldn't keep doing what I was doing and be happy at the same time.

Here is some back story. I studied at Arizona State University and received my Bachelors is Civil Engineering and Masters in Transportation Engineering. I chose my college major during my senior year of high school. I was in an AutoCAD (computer aided drafting) class and I really enjoyed using the software. I wanted to know who used CAD and through research I learned that Civil Engineers used it. Therefore, I selected Civil Engineering as my major for college. I never changed my mind and never second guessed myself. I knew that Civil Engineering was what I wanted to do, so I pursued that goal with everything I had.

During my undergraduate years I also took classes for a minor in Psychology. I was the first Civil Engineering student at the school to ever combine the two disciplines. My academic advisor even said, "We've never had anyone do this before, are you sure? It's easier to get a math minor." I said "Yes, this is what I want to do. I don't want a math minor." As long as I can remember I never let the statement "This is what everyone else is doing" change my mind about what I wanted to do. I view this as a strength of mine, which has led me to where I am now.

I completed six years of engineering school. It wasn't easy and there were times when I wanted to give up and quit, but I didn't. Just before graduating with my Master's Degree, I applied for and interviewed for several positions at engineering companies and received one job offer, so I took it. The offer was for an Airport Engineer In Training positon. During my undergraduate years, I interned for a company that specialized in airport engineering and design and I gained a great deal of experience. I have since learned that the airport engineering network is relatively small and once you're in the network, it is relatively easy to find work and stay in the engineering profession. Anyway, I took the job and worked for the company for just over a year. It wasn't a situation that I wanted to be in. I liked the work, just not the environment.

I looked for different positions for about six months before one became available and I applied for my same position at another company. I received a phone call the same day and an interview at the end of the week. I got that job too! It was an easy transition to the new company. I really fit in with the company culture and I was excited to help them with their proposals and projects.

Soon after switching companies, I took the Professional Engineering exam, passed and received my Professional Engineering License. Applying for the license required quite a bit of paper work, referrals and more paperwork, but I achieved my goal of becoming a Professional Engineer. Yay! So in summary, in 2004 I chose my major and 10 years later I become a Professional and I was done.

That, to me, was a signal for me to move on. I had achieved my goal. Engineering wasn't fulfilling and I wasn't passionate about it. It was just one of my goals and I completed it. Now I was 10 years older with new ideas and new life goals. Yet, at the same time, I found it difficult to accept that I was experiencing new desires for a different life. I was raised to believe that in order to be successful you are supposed to follow this formula:

"go to school" + *"get good grades"* + *"get a job in your profession with benefits"* = *"live a happy successful life"*

By using that definition of success, I should have felt successful, but I didn't. I didn't feel accomplished because I wasn't doing what I really wanted to do with my life. It doesn't matter who you are or what you're doing with your life, if you're not actively doing what you really, really want, then things just don't feel quite right to you. You may experience an unsettling feeling in your body that you can't really explain.

One day I was thinking about how much I wanted my career to be different. I would regularly fantasize (visualize) what I would do with my time if I didn't have to be at a desk all day.

I knew I wanted to pursue a career that allowed me the opportunity to work with people. One day the term "life coach" came to me. Working with and understanding people is my passion. During college, I knew I would apply my true passion in a career someday, I just didn't know how at the time. Well, you've heard the saying, "there is never a perfect time." I was building my career as a Professional Engineer and establishing myself as credible. It definitely wasn't the perfect time for me to explore a career change.

The day I first thought about life coaching, I sent a text message to my mom. It said "What are your thoughts about me being a Life Coach?" and since my mom is my biggest supporter, I knew I would receive constructive feedback. No matter what I want to do, she's always there to provide guidance and support. Her response was "I think you'll be great at it." I researched and learned more about the Life Coaching profession. I found several ways to get certified. It took me about 9 months to decide where to get certified and decide that I was actually going to go back to school to make it happen.

I share this story for two reasons:

1. It doesn't matter how long you have been on one path in your life; it is possible to make changes if you know in your heart that a change needs to be made in order for you to fulfill your desires.

2. Change doesn't happen all at once. After deciding that I would return to school, I continued to work at my engineering job for almost a year before I finally made the decision to leave the engineering profession.

Let's review goals other than career goals. For example: exercising, losing weight, creating more time for yourself in your busy schedule, finding your dream job/career or creating the lifestyle that you want. First, you have to be specific about what you want.

This step is all about identifying your ultimate goal. Identify what you want most in your heart with no limitations or restrictions. Here are a few examples.

- ☐ You want to exercise more
  - What type of exercise?
  - How often?
- ☐ You want to lose weight
  - How much weight?
  - By when?

- ☐ You want more time for yourself
  - How often?
  - What would you do with the time?
- ☐ You want your dream job/career
  - What is it?
  - By when?
- ☐ You want your desired lifestyle
  - What is that lifestyle?
  - By when?

One client, we are going to call her Audrey, has a goal to run her second 5k race. Another client, Cindy, also a pseudo name to protect her identity, has a goal to find a job in healthcare that promotes healthcare as opposed to sick-care where she can financially support herself comfortably.

It doesn't matter what you want, you just have to be able to identify it. And the key is to include as much detail as possible about the goal, desire or outcome. You can also begin to identify when you would like to achieve this desire.

Bob Proctor in the Secret states:

"What do you really want? Sit down and write it out on a piece of paper. Write in the present tense. You might begin by writing "I am so happy and grateful now that …" And then explain how you want your life to be in every area."

The key is to be clear about what you want and to be as specific as possible. Remember in this step there is no judgment. There is no room for second guessing. It is all about just simply writing down what you really, really want for yourself.

Now is the time to get started. You can download the "How to Believe In Yourself Worksheet" at HowToBelieveInYourself.com.

Step 1: Identify Your Goal/Outcome/Desire

What do you really want? This is something that you have reservations about, whether it's a fear of failure, not knowing where to start, or you are doubting yourself about it.

CARMEN PARKS

3 IDENTIFY YOUR SELF-TALK

"Self-talk reflects your inner most feelings" – Asa Don Brown

Step 2 is all about identifying what you are saying to yourself about reaching your greatest goal, desire or outcome. Almost everyone experiences self-talk. Self-talk, is essentially one type of thought. However, I believe that we all have 5 different kinds of thoughts.

1. Planning thoughts
2. Replaying thoughts (memories)
3. Observing thoughts (present moment)
4. Judging thoughts
5. Self-talk thoughts.

Planning thoughts are the thoughts you have when you are thinking about everything you want to do, or everything you have to do. When you are having these thoughts you may also be thinking about all of the details related to the future, who, what, where, when, how and why. These can be very consuming thoughts, and I am personally working on minimizing these thoughts. I am saving them for times when I am purposefully planning something. I have found that at times these thoughts are unnecessary and can get in the way of my observing or present moment thoughts.

Replaying thoughts are essentially memories. These thoughts occur when you are replaying what happened in the past. Sometimes you'll think of ways you could change the past, but usually these thoughts are consumed with replaying your perspective of how events occurred before the present moment. I used to be constantly consumed with replaying embarrassing moments, mentally beating myself up for what I did in the past and honestly, that type of thinking got me nowhere fast.

Observing thoughts are thoughts you have when you're in the present moment. An example of these is "oh, look how blue the sky is" or "that rose smells wonderful." When you are having your observational thoughts you are using one or more of your senses. Sometimes being present is about noticing the things around you and other times it is about just being. When you are fully present there is no room for any of the other types of thoughts.

Judging thoughts are the thoughts you have about other people or events. You may have a tendency to think you know what is best for others around you, or how things 'should' be done. Therefore, in your mind, you may think about what another person might be thinking. You may also have a tendency to decide what another person should be wearing, feeling, thinking or acting. These can sometimes be thoughts that you don't even realize you are having unless you choose to take an outside perspective and catch yourself in the act.

The fifth type of thoughts are your **self-talk thoughts**. These thoughts are about yourself. These can be judgmental thoughts toward yourself or uplifting thoughts, but essentially these are thoughts in which you are speaking directly to yourself about yourself. Self-talk thoughts tell your mind and body how to feel about a certain situation. They can be neutral, they can empower you, or they can defeat you.

In this step of the exercise I want you to become aware of your self-talk thoughts. When you say out loud "I want _____ <*insert answer to Step 1*>" Write down everything that your mind tells you about it. What is your self-talk? What are you saying to yourself? What are you saying about yourself? Write down everything that comes to mind. There are no right or wrong answers, just be completely honest.

Melissa Ng who wanted to be an artist expresses the following self-talk in her article titled "How To Believe In Yourself In The Face of Overwhelming Self-Doubt."

   - Drawing is nice but not necessary.

   - I'll never be as good as the real professionals anyway.

   - I don't even have a degree from an accredited art school

Let's take a look at Audrey's self-talk about running her second 5k.

- I'm afraid to start training because I know I will not commit to a successful training schedule.
- I did not run the entire first 5k last year. I walked much of it.
- I am a year older this year.
- My company is not a sponsor this year and signing up will be out of my pocket this year.
- I am not sure that I can beat last year's time.
- I am afraid that I just won't follow through on the training and on the race.

Now let's review Cindy's self-talk about obtaining a career in healthcare:

- How do I do this?
- All those jobs are taken.
- I'm going to have to learn a new career.
- I probably need experience.
- How much is this going to cost me in time and money?

Finally, I want to give you insight into my self-talk about switching careers from Civil Engineer to Life Coach. These are my thoughts before I made the decision to actually quit my job.

- I don't know anything about Life Coaching.
- I'm so young, most of the life coaches on websites have many years of experience

- Will anyone want to work with me?

- What will my dad think about it?

- How can I possibly quit my job? Nobody just quits their job!

- I replayed my dad's voice "Don't quit a job until you have another one lined up."

Now it's your turn. If you haven't done so already, download the "How to Believe In Yourself Worksheet" at HowToBelieveInYourself.com.

Step 2: Write Down Your Self-Talk

When you say to yourself "I want _____<insert answer to step #1>" Write down everything that your mind tells you about it. What is your self-talk? What are you saying to yourself? What are you saying about yourself? Write down everything that comes to mind. There are no right or wrong answers, just be completely and brutally honest.

CARMEN PARKS

4 IDENTIFY YOUR FEELINGS

"Don't keep all your feelings sheltered – express them. Don't ever let life shut you up." –
Dr. Steve Maraboli

Everyone has feelings. Sometimes you feel things in life and aren't quite able to explain what it is. Sometimes you give feelings or emotions a name. You may call feelings good or you may call them bad. In reality, all feelings are neutral, they are the windows to how and why we take action in life. I also want to point out that all feelings are valid.

Many times we don't consciously know why we do something. However, if we really start to think about it, our actions are the result of feeling a certain way in a particular moment. We may have chosen to take some sort of action or chosen not to take action. The day you start evaluating your feelings, is the day you begin your emotional awareness journey.

According to Cynthia Athina Kemp Scherer who wrote <u>The Art & Technique Of Using Flower Essences</u>,

> *"When we are conscious of what we are feeling and the attitudes we have, we are emotionally aware. When we can distinguish our feelings from the thoughts we have about them, we are emotionally aware."* She goes on to say *"It is important to be aware of our feelings and attitudes because they are often the underlying cause of many of the discomforts in life. When we are aware of what we are feeling, thinking and believing, we are able to interact with these feelings and thoughts."*

Expressing your feelings is about being vulnerable with yourself and sometimes being vulnerable with others. You may have a tendency to suppress your true feelings because you may call them invalid or unreasonable. Someone in your past may have told you that you're not supposed to feel a certain way. You have the right to feel anything and you also have the right to express your feelings. Start by expressing your feelings to yourself and see how it sits with you.

Melissa Ng expressed the following feelings about becoming an artist:

- Afraid of what people would say.
- Afraid everyone would hate her art.
- Afraid of failing as an artist.

My client Audrey, who wants to run her second 5k, developed this list of her feelings:

- I feel like a failure.
- I feel scared.
- I feel immature.
- I feel powerless.
- I feel paralyzed.
- I feel voiceless.
- I feel like I have a headache and that every part of my body hurts.
- I feel defeated.
- I feel broken.
- I feel lost.
- My heart is pounding.
- I feel like I am being held to a standard that I cannot reach.
- I feel like life is pass/fail.

Audrey was very brave to share these feelings with herself and with me. Because she was completely honest, she was able to experience all of the benefits of this exercise.

Cindy was also very brave and experienced these feelings after identifying her self-talk about obtaining a career in the healthcare field.

- I feel a pit in my stomach as my mind starts wrapping around all the specifics.
- I feel frustrated and my heart rate goes up a little.

When I was struggling with the decision to stay in the Civil Engineering field or take the jump into the Wellness field, I had the following feelings.

- I felt stuck as if in a mold
- I felt pressured to stay in my field
- I was frustrated because I was doing what I thought other people wanted me to do.
- I was unhappy and stressed
- I felt out of control
- I felt disconnected
- I felt overwhelmed

In the past I have suffered from severe unhappiness, maybe even depression. I never sought treatment. However, I know that I have a predisposition from family history. I never wanted to admit to anyone what I was feeling because I felt ashamed of the thoughts I was having. From the outside looking in, I now know that my thoughts are what created my unhappiness. Because of my thoughts I would feel:

- Worthless

- Lonely and completely alone

- Unworthy

- Ugly

- Disconnected

Now it is your turn. You have identified your self-talk, it is time for Step 3. Remember to download the "How to Believe In Yourself Worksheet" at HowToBelieveInYourself.com in order to follow along with the book.

Step 3: Write Down Your Feelings

What do you feel when you say the words you wrote in Step 2? Use a thesaurus if you need to find to the correct words that describe your feelings. Write down these feelings and where you feel them in your body. Do you feel them in your head, your throat, your heart, your stomach? Also note what happens to your body. Do your palms get sweaty? Does your heart race? Do you get a tingling sensation?

---

5 EVALUATE YOUR FEELINGS

*"Let your dreams be bigger than your fears, your actions louder than your words and your
faith stronger than your feelings" ~Unknown*

Step 4 is about evaluating your feelings. This may not be something that you do on a regular basis but it can be a practice that is incorporated into your daily thought processes. This evaluation can become part of your self-talk. Recall that self-talk thoughts are about yourself. Evaluating your feelings is about being non-judgmental toward yourself and during this evaluation you will be speaking directly to yourself about yourself.

According to Cynthia Athina Kemp Scherer who wrote The Art & Technique Of Using Flower Essences,

"Many of us, when we look inside, feel things that we would rather not feel. We become aware of thoughts or beliefs that we would rather not have. It takes a tremendous amount of energy to push away these feelings and thoughts. When we can observe and accept that we have them, we have mastered the first steps to creating the reality we want to have."

I chose to include Cynthia's perspective because I completely agree. It is possible to have thoughts, acknowledge or accept them and then we have the opportunity to create new thoughts, if we so choose.

Audrey's evaluation about her feelings related to running her second 5k went something like this:

> *"I logically know that life is not pass/fail and that I can try anything that I want to try. I have support in my life to try anything and I know that nothing bad will happen if I try and do not immediately succeed. There are many things in life that I would love to try and I have never tried."*

Cindy's response during her evaluation step was:

> *"This is definitely not how I wish or want to feel about a life changing goal."*

When I was contemplating the career change I did not formally evaluate my feelings, however I knew that I no longer wanted to feel stuck in a career that I did not want. I was so sick and tired of feeling stuck, stressed and unhappy. My feelings about my career continued to disempower me and those feelings began to take their toll on my personal relationships, especially the one with my partner. I was constantly stressed, irritable and inconsolable. I couldn't quite explain what was wrong when others wanted to help me. Since I felt out of control in the area of my career, I ultimately tried to control other areas of my life, leading to more heartache for all because I ended up pushing people away.

Eventually, my partner made it clear that our happiness was more important than my paycheck. This external support was key for me and it was incredibly liberating. I was able to mentally snap myself out of my excuses for staying stuck and I was able to come to terms with quitting my job.

Paul C. Brunson wrote "10 Things You Must Stop Doing Today To Believe In Yourself," His number eight is:

"8) Going At It Alone. I write frequently about the importance of surrounding yourself with as many good people as possible. But let's face it, sometimes the well for good friends is dry. That said, I don't believe we were put on earth to be alone with our ideas. You must find your one supporter! When I decided to become a matchmaker, everyone told me I was crazy but I was able to find support from my wife. All you need is one person to have your back and it makes your belief infinitely easier."

As you go through this process, I invite you to think about who can possibly be your supporter. Who will have your back? Recognize that you may not have met this person yet. Also, know that the people who tell you that your desire is impossible, are not usually your biggest supporters.

Since formally creating this process, whenever I'm feeling stressed, overwhelmed and unhappy, I now know to take a step back and reevaluate the situation. I ask myself these questions: "What I am doing?" "Is this what I want to be doing?" If so, then I ask "Is this how I want to feel about it?" When I realize that I don't want to have those feelings of disempowerment, discouragement or helplessness, I use my emotionally freeing acronym (K.I.S.S.) to snap me out of my untrue thoughts.

Clients I've worked with tend to continuously play over and over in their heads everything that is not working in their lives. Or clients imagine various scenarios of what could possibly go wrong only to find that yet again things turned out the way they had imagined and they weren't delightfully surprised with a different happy ending.

The thoughts you are having, which you identified in Step 2 (Chapter 3), are the reason for your feelings. And these feelings will not go away as long as you continue to have those particular thoughts.

Now it is time for you to evaluate your feelings. You can download the "How to Believe In Yourself Worksheet" at HowToBelievInYourself.com.

Step 4: Evaluate Your Feelings

Now is the time to take a non-judgmental perspective. Before doing this step. Sit back, close your eyes and take 5 deep breaths. Now, decide if you like the feelings you are experiencing. Answer the question: "Is this how I truly want to feel about reaching my goal?

---

6 WRITE NEW FEELINGS

"Whenever I'm feeling good, I'm attracting good" ~Unknown

Step 5 presents an amazing opportunity to choose how you want to feel instead of the feelings you identified in Step 3. This is where you have the opportunity to be creative and open to everything that is possible. Believing in yourself is a feeling. If you want to believe in yourself, what other emotions would you like to experience?

Melissa Ng suggests the following:

"Trust and love yourself. You probably spend more time being your own worst enemy instead of being your own best friend. But you deserve to treat yourself better." She goes on to say *"Give yourself permission to try…and try again. Self-doubt never disappears. Over time, you just get better at dealing with it."*

Melissa brings up a couple of very important points. First, she suggests that you trust and love yourself. This is something that is not always easy and may not come natural. Sometimes it is so much easier to put yourself down and create excuses. I also love that Melissa suggests giving yourself permission to try. If you don't try, you will never really know what you are capable of accomplishing.

Audrey, our 5k runner, listed the following desired feelings for Step 5.

- I want to be more brave.
- I wish that I could, and would, try more things knowing that life is not pass/fail.
- I wish I could, and would, laugh at early attempts to learn new things and learn and grow and try and try and try and enjoy trying
- I want to learn to enjoy the trying... The experiencing of new things, instead of seeing and experiencing everything as a test of pass/fail.

Cindy identified the following as her desired feelings:

- I want to feel excitement
- I want to be overjoyed to the point that I can't contain it or stop it.

The new feelings that I wished to experience about my career change were:

- freedom
- a feeling of endless possibilities

- excited about my everyday work
- a sense of knowing that I was doing the right thing
- a sense of peace
- unconstrained

Believing in yourself is a choice. As stated earlier in the book, if you believe you can, you will, if you believe you can't, you won't. What have you been believing all of these years? Louise Hay writes the following in her book Heal Your Body:

"How often have we said "That's the way I am," or "That's the way it is." What we're really saying is that it is what we "believe to be true for us." Usually what we believe is only someone else's opinion that we've accepted and incorporated into our own belief system. It fits in with other things that we believe." She goes on to say *"Life experiences mirror our beliefs."*

Now it is your turn to write down new feelings. Download the "How to Believe In Yourself Worksheet" at HowToBelieveInYourself.com.

Step 5: Write New Feelings

Now is the time to take a non-judgmental perspective. Before doing this step. Sit back, close your eyes and take 5 deep breaths. Now, decide if you like the feelings you are experiencing. Answer the question: "Is this how I truly want to feel about reaching my goal?

CARMEN PARKS

7 CREATE NEW SELF-TALK

"The only person who can pull me down is myself, and I'm not going to let myself pull me down anymore." ~ C. JoyBell C.

Now that you've identified the feelings you wish to experience when you think about your chosen goal/outcome/desire, it is time to identify the words that inspire those feelings inside of you. Recall that in Step 2 you wrote down words, your self-talk, and in Step 3 you identified the feelings you experienced as a result of those words. Now we are working backwards. You now have your list of desired feelings or emotions. In Step 6 you have the opportunity to develop new words that can become a response to those internal or external naysayers. These words inspire your desired feelings.

Ramit Sethi, creator of the company IWT and author of the book <u>I Will Teach You To Be Rich</u>, had several followers ask him how he achieved his goals. His response was that he started to believe in himself. In his blog he outlines four ways that he started believing in himself. Here is his third step:

"3. Handle naysayers. A lot of people told me (the idea of my company), IWT, was stupid, the name was stupid, and why should anyone listen to me? Honestly, it hurt, especially when I was starting out and wasn't sure I actually had a good response. And I tried every horrible tactic. I argued with them. I ignored them. I challenged them. All stupid. The best technique was co-opting their criticism by saying, "You know what, you might be right! I have no idea if this is going to work. But I figure I have to give it a shot, right? If you were me, what would you do?" The deeper part of this was truly mastering my own personal psychology to know how to push through the tough parts."

In Ramit's article about how to deal with critics, he suggests:

"I recommend you remind yourself of this: Opinions are cheap. Everyone will have them, because it's easy to point out things you're doing wrong, or ways you "should" think about things." He goes on to say *"Always ask yourself: Is this advice-giver in the situation I want to be in?"*

Your biggest critic may also be yourself. You may hear other people's opinions and in the past you might have chosen to also make those your opinions. Now you might be replaying other people's words as your own thoughts. Well, now is the time to really create your own thoughts. These are thoughts that you want to think about while working to reach your goals.

One suggestion for helping you overcome your fears and self-doubts is to catch yourself in the act. Recognize when you say "I can't do it" or "I've failed before." When you feel the defeating energy build up in your body, you know it is time for a different perspective. You can change those statements into "I can't do it yet" or "I've failed before, but I will try again." Notice the energy shift in your body when you rephrase self-defeating statements in to self-empowering statements. All situations where you see obstacles can also be seen as opportunities for growth and development. Do you believe that you deserve the chance to take advantage of those opportunities?

The above examples of statements depict the difference between reactive language and proactive language. In Steven Covey's book <u>The 7 Habits of Highly Effective People</u>, he breaks down the difference between reactive and proactive people.

> *"Our language, for example, is a very real indicator of the degree to which we see ourselves as proactive people. The language of reactive people absolves them of responsibility."*
>
> *"A serious problem with reactive language is that it becomes a self-fulfilling prophecy. People become reinforced in the paradigm that they are determined, and they produce evidence to support the belief. They feel increasingly victimized and out of control, not in charge of their life or their destiny. They blame outside forces – other people, circumstances, even the stars for their own situation."*
>
> *"In the great literature of all progressive societies, love is a verb. Reactive people make it a feeling. They're driven by feelings….. Proactive people make love a verb. Love is something you do: the sacrifices you make, the giving of self, like a mother bringing a newborn into the world."*

To expand upon Steven Covey's perspective, we all have the opportunity to choose our actions. Reactive people believe the actions they are taking are because of an external circumstance or event, ultimately leading to feeling out of control with a pre-determined situation. Proactive people take deliberate actions because they want to, which leads to feeling more in control, allowing them to know that their actions are leading to their desired situation.

In my life, I am the overachiever who received almost all A's in Middle School, High School and College. My school experiences taught me that I could achieve an A grade in every class if I did the work that was required. The times that I really wanted an A and didn't get it was because I know I didn't put in the work to get the A. I put in the work to receive a lesser grade. In these situations, I was honest with myself. It's not that the teacher gave me a lower grade. It's that I didn't earn a higher grade. I have always had a tendency to take the proactive perspective to life. I also see this as one of my strengths.

Step 6 is all about choosing words that allow you to take a proactive response to reaching your goals.

Audrey completed Step 6 and created a list of words that inspire her desired feelings toward completing her second 5k race.

- I am brave
- I will try one new activity per month or per year
- Start slowly
- I am confident
- Review things that I have done that are brave
- Remind myself that the world did not open and swallow me whole when I failed
- Feelings are just feelings, they are not facts

- Feelings will pass
- I am not my feelings
- My self-worth is not based upon my latest attempt to try something new
- I am strong

Cindy also created new words for her self-talk, which inspired her to take action toward her goal of working in healthcare.

- Determination
- Drive
- Overcome
- Focused

As you can see there is no one way to complete this step. You know what is best for you at this time and you now have the opportunity to decide which words or phrases will best serve you and inspire you toward your chosen goal/outcome/desire.

Words that I currently use are:

- You've got this
- My short yet powerful acronym: K.I.S.S (Keep It Super Simple)
- Internal power
- Feel it first
- One thing at a time

We all have the power to choose our thoughts. Our thoughts propel us towards our goals or hold us back with excuses. I have used my thoughts to empower me and I have used my thoughts to strip away all self-worth. The interesting thing is that we tend to believe our thoughts whether they are true or not.

When I was working to overcome my very unhappy mental situation, it wasn't easy and it took practice. However, now I work hard to only use my thoughts to build myself up. We all have too many critics in this world, there is no reason for us to also constantly criticize ourselves. Who is going to empower us if we don't choose to do it ourselves?

Now it is your turn to write down all of the words that inspire your new feelings. Download the "How to Believe In Yourself Worksheet" at HowToBelieveInYourself.com.

Step 6: Create New Self-Talk

Looking at your desired feelings listed in Step 5, write on your list the words that you can include in your new self-talk that will cause you to experience your desired feelings.

---

8 CREATE AFFIRMATIONS OR DECLARATIONS

"Believe it can be done. When you believe something can be done, really believe, your mind will find the ways to do it. Believing a solution paves the way to solution." ~David J. Schwartz, The Magic of Thinking Big

Step 7 is where you are going to create your own affirmation. You probably have already heard about affirmations. Maybe you've already used them in the past. Other words for affirmation are mantra or declaration. Everyone is motivated by something different. Whatever descriptive word works best for you, please choose to use it throughout this chapter. I will be using either the word mantra or affirmation depending on the situation.

Affirmations are not designed to overpower or get rid of any other thoughts. They are designed to partner with your other thoughts as you practice new thoughts. Your default self-talk is something you learned over time. It has become a habit. The great thing about habits is that they can be changed if you want them to change. If you don't like your self-talk, this is an opportunity to really take a good look at it and decide what you would rather think instead.

My first memory of using visualizations to achieve a goal was when I was 5 or 6 years old. I had a dream that I was riding my two wheeled bicycle without the training wheels. The next day I was completely convinced that I was able to ride the bike. I talked about it all day to anyone who would listen to me. I never got the sense that anyone really believed me, but I kept talking anyway. After school, my neighbor friend had a bike that I could use and sure enough, I was able to ride the two-wheeler, just as I had in my dream! The reason I share this story, is because at an early age, I had confidence in myself as well as confidence in my own feelings and in my own beliefs, even when others doubted me.

My second memory of using visualizations to achieve a goal was in eighth grade. One of my sisters was in sixth grade and we were both on the cross country running team. We raced against other schools and throughout the season, my younger sister kept getting closer and closer to finishing the races at the same time as I did. In one race we finished at almost the same time. The next race was the championship race. My parents, the cross country coach and our teammates continued to tell me that she was going to finish the race ahead of me. They also said that she was a better runner than I was. But before the race, I chose to be sure that she would not finish before me.

I made up a mantra (I didn't know it was a mantra at the time) but every time I ran in practice, leading up to the big race, I repeated the mantra over and over in my head. And during the race, that mantra kept me motivated and pushed me all the way to the finish line. Sure enough, my younger sister was nowhere near me. I was way ahead and in my mind there was absolutely no way she was going to finish the race ahead of me.

I would share this mantra, however, unfortunately I do not remember the words. The important fact is that it worked!

In summary, to prepare for the race, I visualized myself placing ahead of her in the race and I used the mantra to keep me motivated. On race day, that's exactly what happened. I was completely consumed with making sure what I wanted would actually come true. At no time did I listen to what others were saying or what anyone else thought about the situation. I was so focused on staying ahead of her in the race that there was no room in my brain for other people's opinions.

At that time I had no idea what I was doing or how I was doing it but looking back, it was a combination of determination and visualization which led me to believe in myself no matter what else was going on that day. I now use mantras, affirmations and visualizations to help me achieve all of my goals.

Now, whenever I have an upcoming race, I set a goal, create a visualization and use a mantra. I use the mantra by replaying it over and over and over in my head to help me reach my goal. What do you keep replaying over and over and over in your head? Is it motivating you or holding you back?

Melissa Ng suggests the following as a tip for believing in yourself:

"Recall your successes. This one is tough. When you're down, you'll more easily remember the bad instead of the good. And oftentimes, the "rah-rah" pep talk just doesn't cut it. So, I suggest writing a list. Grab a piece of paper or small notebook, or open a blank document. Now write down your successes, big or small"

Nadia Goodman wrote an article titled "Fake It Until You Make It, How to Believe In Yourself When You Don't Feel Worthy." Her last and fourth step is:

"4. See "faking it" as a skill. We all have moments when we need to fake confidence or sell an idea that was thrown together at the last minute. In those moments, impostors tend to focus on thoughts like, "that was all an act," which leaves them feeling fraudulent. But knowing how to appear confident is a valuable asset in any job. "It's a skill to be able to walk in and act like you know what you're doing even if you don't," Young says. Allowing yourself to build and applaud that skill -- without practicing any intentional harm or deceit -- will help you feel credible even when you're out of your comfort zone."

So what can you say to yourself to help you fully believe? What statements empower you to start believing in yourself to get you to 'fake it until you make it'?

Audrey came up with the following affirmations to keep her motived toward her goal of running her second 5k race:

- I am strong
- I am a survivor
- I am brave
- I have been through bigger challenges
- I can do it
- I am more than enough
- I am a great role model

54

- Do it with grace
- Do it happy
- It is a choice
- Choose wisely
- Just today

These statements help Audrey bring herself back into the present moment and remind her that she already has all of these wonderful qualities. She also knows that she doesn't have to run the race today, she just has to think about and start taking action today.

Cindy also developed a great list to keep her motivated and taking action toward her goal of a career in healthcare:

- Focus on where I see myself in a new career
- Meet with a counselor to assess an education program towards health education
- Stay positive and remember it's a journey that will take time

Cindy, too recognized that everything doesn't happen overnight. As she stated, "It's a journey."

I currently use countless affirmations depending on the situation. For training and running races I repeat over and over again the following mantras/affirmations, depending on how I'm feeling.

- I am capable
- You've done this before
- Just one more mile
- You've got this
- I am strong
- Healthy, strong

When I am mentally working on business or relationship struggles, I use one simple phrase: K.I.S.S. Keep It Super Simple. I know that the moment I start to overthink a situation, I get overwhelmed and I notice the stress and anxiety building up in my body like a tight hold that won't let go. I start taking short breaths and can't quite seem to calm my mind. This feeling in my body reminds me that I'm not keeping it simple and I just tell myself to K.I.S.S. Keep It Super Simple. Nearly immediately I can feel my body begin to relax and I am able to stop the non-stop thoughts and start back at the beginning.

I ask myself: "What do I really, really want?" That is when I start this process. This is not a "one-time, then you're done" type of process. This is something you can use every time you start to feel those unpleasant feelings in your body. Those feelings you identified in Step 3 will be your sign. You will know that it is time to reevaluate, choose how you want to feel and then create an affirmation to guide you.

When you believe this affirmation it will change the way you feel. I believe in the law of attraction and according to the writers of The Secret, thoughts lead to feelings and feelings are what attract desires and events into our lives. All feelings have the power of attraction. Recall that your feeling are your internal power.

Have you ever noticed that people who complain about all of the things that are going wrong in their lives, tend to consistently experience more and more things about which to complain. The law of attraction works both ways. Your feelings give energy to the situation. What do you want to attract into your life?

Congratulations! You have reached the last step! Download the "How to Believe In Yourself Worksheet" at HowToBelieveInYourself.com to complete this process.

Step 7: Create Affirmations or Declarations

Using the words you listed in Step 6, create affirmations / mantras / declarations that will empower your desired feelings. These statements can keep you focused and working toward your goal / outcome / desire.

---

9 DO'S AND DON'TS

"There will be haters, there will be doubters, there will be non-believers, and then there will be you proving them wrong." ~Unknown

Congratulations you've created an affirmation that is going to keep you motivated toward your goal. Now, you may be thinking, "Ok, I do feel better but I still have some fears and doubts." That's ok. This is a process and change doesn't happen overnight. You've just learned to recognize thoughts that lead to the feelings that hold you back. You've also learned how to choose new feelings and new thoughts so that you can refocus and feel mentally more capable of reaching your goal.

Now that you've completed all seven steps, here are a few Do's and Don'ts for practicing this method:

- Do practice visualizing your desired future.
- Do recognize when you are falling back into old thought patterns.
- Do remember that new feelings and thoughts feel strange. That's fine.

- Do know that the more you chose thoughts and feelings that empower you, the more it will become habit.

- Don't start mentally beating yourself up for having thoughts that disempower you.

- After having the disempowering thought, mentally or verbally state an affirmation that counteracts that automatic (old) thought.

- Do realize that thoughts are choices. Beliefs are choices. You get to choose what you believe and it's time to start believing in yourself.

- Don't name call. Words such as "Bad" are a huge pitfall. Just notice your thoughts without labeling or judgment and appreciate yourself for noticing.

Let's address each, one at a time:

Do practice visualizing your desired future. Throughout this book, I have talked about how visualizations have helped me to reach my goals. Chances are you already use visualizations, you just may not have purposely used them to imagine yourself reaching your goals. Now that you know what you really, really want and you know how you want to feel about it, it's time to create a picture of your desired outcome in your mind. See yourself doing whatever it is you want to do. Use your senses. What do you see, feel, smell, hear or taste? Who is there with you? This is your imagination and anything is possible. Be as descriptive as you can and if you want to, write it all down for future reference.

Do recognize when you are falling back into old thought patterns. Recall all those feelings you identified in Step 3. When these feelings begin to return, you will know that you are falling back into old thought patterns.

However, now you know how to get yourself out of those thought patterns. Quickly go through this process. Take a minute and write down or think about how you would rather feel instead and create an affirmation to bring your emotions back to where you want them to be. Remember, your thoughts are a choice, even if and when you are having default thoughts. You have the opportunity to change your thoughts, if you so choose.

Do remember that new feelings and thoughts feel strange, that's fine. If you haven't practiced changing your thoughts before, it will feel different but as your thoughts change, your feelings change and then the way you experience the world around you changes. It takes practice just like any new skill. Don't expect yourself to be a master right away (but if you are, that's cool too!). Be patient with yourself and keep at it because before you know it, you will have new default thoughts.

Do know that the more you choose thoughts and feelings that empower you the more it will become a habit. The opposite is also true. The more you choose thoughts that disempower you the more it will become a habit. Choose right now how you want to feel. Do you want to feel afraid, worried, apprehensive or do you want to feel motivated, excited and passionate? Thoughts lead to feelings. Today is the day to start choosing the thoughts that lead to the feelings and emotions you desire.

Don't start mentally beating yourself up for having thoughts that disempower you. Recognize that you had that thought, because it is ok to have them. Now you've decided that you are only going to have thoughts that empower you because you think, "Why would I want to feel down, scared and afraid to reach my goals?" Well, you can't turn those feelings off, not forever. It's natural for our brains to protect us from something new and unfamiliar. Our brains are hard wired to keep us safe and anything new and unfamiliar can be seen as a potential threat to our wellbeing. When this occurs our brains automatically alert our bodies of some impending danger. That is why we sometimes experience fear. In evolutionary terms, it is "dangerous" to be out-casted from the "colony".

In general, we all can admit that we want approval and support from our peers. If we start to make a decision that we think may be against the "norm" then there is potential ridicule or we may even lose friends and might possibly be labeled as an outcast. Hundreds of years ago, outcast members of society did not live as long. Acceptance by one's community was vital to living a healthy and long life for many reasons. Therefore, a portion of our brain is hardwired to believe that in order to survive we need to stay the same and make no changes to our lives. That way we can maintain our status quo with our friends and neighbors. This is our instinctual brain at work. Its only goal is survival. Since we are no longer concerned with simple survival, we can choose to also thrive. If you choose to thrive, then you know what to do next. Accept those thoughts and then say, "Well no, I get to choose new thoughts." Even if it's scary, choose new thoughts. This is when growth will be at its greatest speed.

After having a thought that disempowers you, mentally or verbally state an affirmation that counteracts that automatic (old) thought. This is why you developed affirmations in Step 7. And you can continuously create any affirmation you need to get you through the day, an event or even to keep you inspired toward your intended goal. Depending on my goal for the day or a training program, I choose the affirmation that keeps me motivated and moving in the moment. You can do the same. Affirmations are personal and are designed specifically for you and the way you think. Know that your affirmations may not work for someone else and their affirmations may not work for you and that is fine. We are each coming from a different background and are reaching different goals for different reasons.

Do realize that thoughts are choices. Beliefs are choices. You choose what you believe and it's time to start believing in yourself. Do you remember the moment that you started doubting yourself? Maybe it was something someone else said, maybe it was a personal disappointment because you didn't reach your goal and were embarrassed or humiliated. There was some external event that caused you to change your internal environment. And that's normal. Believing in yourself is a feeling that comes from within. No one else can make you, or cause you, to have that feeling. You have the opportunity to choose whether or not you want to believe in yourself and whether or not you want to do the work to combat those old automatic thoughts.

Don't name call. Words such as "bad" are a huge pitfall. Just notice your thoughts without labeling or judgment and appreciate yourself for noticing. We all want to be accepted and positively regarded by others. But does that mean we have to put ourselves down? That seems rather silly, doesn't it? It is not productive to talk down to yourself and talk badly about yourself. You may have gossiped about another person in your life, usually it's something not so nice. Have you ever had the thought, "Geez, I wish they didn't talk about me like this behind my back"?

Maybe you are already saying those things to yourself in the mirror. Why aren't we nice to ourselves? What if your best friend said those things about you out loud to other people? What if your best friend said those things to your face? Would you be embarrassed? Would you feel betrayed? Would you be offended? Then why is ok for you to say them to yourself? What if you only said empowering statements to yourself? What if you only said things that you wish other people would say about you? How uplifting would that be?

If you do have a thought that disempowers you and makes you feel poorly about yourself, that's fine. No one is perfect. Once you have the thought, you have an opportunity to recognize it and change it. Be patient with yourself. Maybe you want to sit with it for a minute and figure out why you automatically have that thought. Was it something someone said to you years ago? Identifying where it came from makes it easier to release it and replace it. As Byron Katie suggestions, first ask yourself "Is it true?" Then ask yourself, "Am I sure?"

Changing habits takes time. You are far ahead of where you were before you started reading this book. Be patient with yourself and trust that when you believe in yourself you are unstoppable.

10 THE NEXT STEPS

"Life is short, fragile and does not wait for anyone. There will NEVER be a perfect time to pursue your dreams and goals. " ~ Unknown

So what's next? You have your goal identified, you've taken steps to identify thoughts and feelings that are no longer serving you and you have even chosen new thoughts and feelings that motivate you to take action! You have probably thought about the next steps. Well, for any goal to be reached, action must be taken. Where do you start? When do you start? How long will it take you to get to where you want to be? Who is going to hold you accountable along the way? I invite you to visit my website to download a complimentary step-by-step guide for setting SMART Goals. This is the second step in reaching any goal.

Visit ImproveYourGoalSettingSkills.com to learn more.

ABOUT THE AUTHOR

Carmen is a Civil Engineer turned Holistic Life Coach. She is passionate
about empowering others to always believe in themselves. Through
coaching, she helps clients become "unstuck" from default thought
patterns. Carmen believes that changing thought patterns is the first step
toward improving health and wellness. The next steps are
about addressing nutrition, exercise and spiritual alignment, all of which
help fuel a happy, healthy lifestyle.

When Carmen left engineering a few things remained the same. One of
them was running. To her, nothing feels better than finishing a race that
requires more mental effort than physical effort. The first thing needed in
order to cross a finish line is to believe in oneself. Carmen regularly states:
"No matter what you want out of life, you are never going to have it if you
don't truly believe you can do what it takes to get it."

Made in the USA
Charleston, SC
01 March 2015